THE
Bride and Groom
HANDBOOK

PRESENTED TO

PHYLLIS AND MICHAEL

BY

UNCLE DON AND AUNT EDITH

DATE

25 SHEVAT 5754
FEBRUARY 6, 1994

D1113351

THE
Bride and Groom
HANDBOOK

RABBI RONALD H. ISAACS

BEHRMAN HOUSE

Feelings are "entertained": love comes to pass.
Feelings dwell in man; but man dwells in his love.
That is no metaphor, but the actual truth.
Love does not cling to the *I* in such a way as to have
the *Thou* only for its "content," its object;
but love is *between I* and *Thou* ... Love is
responsibility of an *I* for a *Thou*.
FROM *I AND THOU* BY MARTIN BUBER

PROJECT EDITOR: RUBY G. STRAUSS
BOOK DESIGN: BARBARA HUNTLEY
COVER PHOTO: MARC CHAGALL:
"THE BRANCH"/FOUR BY FIVE
COPYRIGHT © BY RONALD H. ISAACS
PUBLISHED BY BEHRMAN HOUSE, INC.
235 WATCHUNG AVENUE, WEST ORANGE, NJ 07052
ISBN 0-87441-476-8
MANUFACTURED IN THE UNITED STATES OF AMERICA

CONTENTS

PREFACE

THE phone rings. An excited voice announces, "Rabbi, great news! We're engaged to be married, and we want you to perform the wedding ceremony."

Such calls are always filled with joy and the anticipation of an event that will be one of the most important in every couple's life, just as it is in yours. Emotions run high as you chart the course of a new life together.

One of the first subjects to command attention, of course, is the planning of the wedding itself—the ceremony that will solemnize your feelings for one another, and the festivities which will celebrate your union.

You will soon discover that your marriage is not only the union of two individuals, but indeed the joining of two families. This is a good time to set a pattern of compromise; for the wedding day will pass, but your life together will span the decades. Don't allow minor details to provide the basis for future discord. Rather, let your wedding day be just the first of many joyous occasions celebrated together by your two newly joined families. Let it be the cornerstone of a long and happy life based on trust, love and companionship.

The specific choices you will make concerning your wedding day are many. I would like to outline some of the questions frequently asked by engaged couples. I hope the answers will help you make your plans, as well as stimulate discussions between the two of you. Perhaps they will also lead you to additional questions which your own rabbi can answer.

The choices you make will shape your wedding day into a truly memorable and personal experience. The unique customs and traditions of our Jewish heritage can make it a spiritual and beautiful experience for all those who share it with you.

I hope that this handbook will help you make knowledgeable choices as you plan the details of your wedding day.

Congratulations! *Mazal Tov!*

RON ISAACS

CHECKLIST

This list will help you to keep track of your wedding plans.

Date of our wedding ⸺⸺⸺⸺⸺⸺⸺⸺⸺
Officiating clergy ⸺⸺⸺⸺⸺⸺⸺⸺⸺⸺
Our wedding will take place at ⸺⸺⸺⸺⸺⸺
Our reception will take place at ⸺⸺⸺⸺⸺⸺
Our meeting with the Rabbi will take place on ⸺⸺

☐ We have ordered our wedding invitations

☐ We have selected our wedding ring(s)

☐ We have chosen our wedding apparel

☐ We have selected our *ḥuppah*

☐ We have selected our *ketubah*

Our witnesses will be ⸺⸺⸺⸺⸺⸺⸺⸺ ,

⸺⸺⸺⸺⸺⸺⸺⸺⸺⸺⸺⸺⸺⸺

We have chosen our attendants:

The best man is ⸺⸺⸺⸺⸺⸺⸺⸺⸺⸺
The maid/matron of honor is ⸺⸺⸺⸺⸺⸺

☐ We have chosen the musical selections

☐ We have taken our blood tests and applied for the civil
license

☐ We have been tested for genetic diseases

☐ We have arranged for an *aufruf*

"I will betroth you with righteousness,
with justice, with love and compassion."

HOSEA 2:21

How does Jewish tradition relate to us as an engaged couple?

THE importance of marriage in the Jewish tradition is summed up in the Talmudic statement that when one marries, one becomes a complete person. Marriage is regarded as the ideal state. In the very first book of the Bible, God tells Adam that it is not good for man to live alone.

Marriage is considered a *mitzvah,* a divine commandment. When a Jewish couple marries, it becomes possible for them to fulfill Judaism's first Biblical obligation—"be fruitful and multiply." A Jewish marriage celebrates the creation of a new Jewish family. With the arrival of its first child, that family becomes God's partner in the ongoing process of creation. For this reason the Zohar says, "God is constantly creating new worlds by causing marriages to take place."

It is interesting to note that there is no single, precise word for marriage in Hebrew. The Bible only speaks of "taking a wife." Many years ago our sages used the word *kiddushin* (sanctification) to mean marriage. This expression reflects the spirituality and holiness that are an integral part of the husband/wife relationship.

In Jewish literature God is often portrayed as a *shadḥan,* a matchmaker.

A rabbinic parable describes a confrontation between a skeptical Roman matron and Rabbi Yose ben Chalafta. The woman asked the rabbi, "In how many days did God create the world?"

"In six days," the rabbi answered.

"What has your God been doing since then?" she asked.

The rabbi replied, "God makes marriages, assigning this man to that woman, and this woman to that man."

The story goes on to tell how the matron, unimpressed, quickly married off all her household slaves, two by two, claiming that she could do the same as Rabbi Yose's God. The very next day the villa resounded with complaints and protests from the newly married couples. Finally the matron relented. She summoned Rabbi Yose and admitted, "There is no God like your God."

Judaism has always viewed marriage as a sacred agreement between two loving companions. This exalted partnership has even been compared to the covenantal bond which God established with the Jewish people when they were chosen to be God's treasured nation.

Of all the happy occasions in the Jewish life cycle, the wedding is the celebration of celebrations—the *simḥa* of *simḥas.* The consecration of a marriage is such cause for rejoicing that no other festivity is allowed to interfere with it. Throughout the ages the wedding ceremony was an occasion to be shared by the entire Jewish community, and it was the community's responsibility to do everything possible to ensure the happiness of every bride and groom. Since antiquity, the celebration of a marriage has included music, feasting, dancing and jesting. In fact, in many communities of old the festivities continued for an entire week! Even today, many traditional couples celebrate each evening of the first week of their marriage in the company of friends and family.

Your wedding day will likely be the quintessential event in your life. It is a consecration, a sanctification of life itself. The Ba'al Shem Tov, founder of Hassidism, said it well: "From every human being there rises a light that reaches to heaven. When two souls are destined to find each other, their streams of light flow together, and a single brighter light goes forth from their united being."

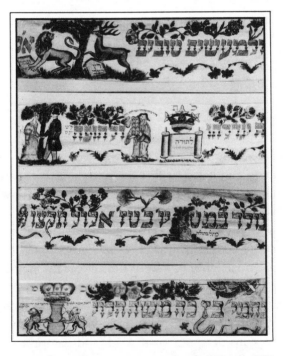

In Germany, it was customary to cut a baby's swaddling cloth into four parts and to sew them together to form a wimpel *(Torah binder). Embroidered or painted on the* wimpel *were the child's name, date of birth, and the wish that he "may grow up to the study of Torah, to the nuptial canopy and to good deeds." Painted linen Torah Binder for Nehemiah Halevi, Germany 1836*

"May there soon be heard the voice of
rejoicing and the voice of gladness."

SHEVA BRACHOT

How shall we select the date of our wedding?

As you begin to plan for your wedding day, you will soon find that every decision seems to depend upon another. The first thing to do is to choose a date. Once you establish the exact date and time for your wedding, other decisions will be easier for you to make.

How you choose your wedding date will, to some extent, reflect your personal priorities. If it is important for you to have a particular rabbi or cantor officiate at the wedding, you will have to take into account their schedules and prior commitments. Similarly, you may want to consider the availability of your close family and special friends. In addition, it is important to consider your own work and vacation schedules. The season of the year, climate and weather are other factors you might consider.

Jewish tradition also places some limitations on the choice of a wedding date. For instance, weddings are never held on the Sabbath or on Festivals so that we do not mix—and consequently dilute—each joyous occasion. In addition, marriage is considered a legal transaction, and business transactions are not permitted on the Sabbath and Festivals. Days which commemorate tragic events in Jewish history are also not appropriate times for a marriage celebration (*Sephirah Period, The Three Weeks, Minor Fast Days*). There is some variation in the observance of these special days, so be sure to consult with your rabbi before the final selection of your wedding date.

It is Jewish custom to count seven weeks from the second day of Passover to Shavuot. These 49 days are known as the Sephirah Period. *Omer Counter made by Maurice Mayer, goldsmith by appointment to Napoleon III.*

"When husband and wife are worthy
the *Shechinah* abides with them."

SOTAH, 17a

How shall we choose the location for our wedding?

THERE are no Jewish laws restricting the selection of the location for your wedding and reception. There are, however, some guidelines to consider.

There is probably no finer way to highlight the spiritual nature of your wedding than to hold the ceremony in a synagogue sanctuary. This setting provides an aura of sanctity and spirituality. If you have a personal attachment to your synagogue, you will feel especially comfortable in the familiar surroundings which will call to mind other happy celebrations held there.

If you do decide to get married in a synagogue, the synagogue's social hall is an attractive and convenient choice for the reception. However, hotels and catering establishments are certainly viable alternatives.

Outdoor weddings, too, are not only acceptable but indeed rooted in Jewish tradition. Customarily, outdoor weddings, especially those held in the evening, were considered to bring good luck because the bride and groom could see the stars which would remind them of God's promise to Abraham that the Jewish people would be as prolific as the stars in the sky.

Weddings held in the home of the bride or groom have always been in fashion. A wedding at home can add an atmosphere of warmth and intimacy and is ideal if you want an informal ceremony in an intimate setting.

No matter which location you choose, it is important to consider your own as well as your guests' comfort and travel arrangements. If any of the guests are elderly or handicapped, you should check into the accessibility of the location (e.g. ramps and/or elevators).

Your choice of where to be married might well be influenced by the kind of cuisine available at a particular place. Because the Jewish wedding is considered a religious as well as a social occasion, the meal served at its celebration is an integral part of the ritual, a *se'udat mitzvah* (ritually prescribed feast). It is, therefore, altogether proper and fitting for the wedding feast to be a kosher meal. You will be happy to find that the inclusion of a kosher meal in your wedding festivities will add an extra measure of spirituality and Jewish flavor to your very important day.

"Set me as a seal upon your heart."
SONG OF SONGS 8:6

Who will officiate at our wedding?

AN ordained rabbi or cantor may perform a wedding that is recognized both Jewishly and civilly. If your family is affiliated with a synagogue, your own rabbi is the best choice. A rabbi who knows you and your family will add a personal touch of warmth to the ceremony.

If your family is unaffiliated, seek out people whose opinion you trust to help you find appropriate clergy. If you are a student, the campus Hillel rabbi might be the logical choice.

You may, of course, have more than one officiant. It is not unusual to have both the bride and the groom represented by each family's rabbi and/or cantor. It is accepted protocol for the host rabbi to contact the visiting clergy prior to the wedding day so that they may plan the ceremony together.

You should arrange a meeting with the rabbi well before your wedding day. Come prepared with questions to discuss. Here are some points you might like to discuss with the rabbi:

- The format of the ceremony, and how much Hebrew will be incorporated into it;
- The inclusion of personal elements in the ceremony (poems, readings, your own vows);
- The honorarium or charitable contribution for the services of the clergy;

- The kind of *ketubah* (marriage contract) the rabbi uses. Come prepared with your Hebrew names and your parents' Hebrew names. The rabbi will need this information to complete the *ketubah*.

The rabbi will be able to tell you where to apply for the civil marriage license and when and where to take the required blood tests.

Increasingly, couples are deciding to be tested for Tay Sachs disease and other genetic disorders to which some Jewish populations seem statistically susceptible. You might want to discuss this with the rabbi as well.

"God has dressed me with garments of exultation...
As a bridegroom puts on a priestly diadem,
and a bride adorns herself with jewels."

ISAIAH 61:10

Are there guidelines to follow when choosing our wedding apparel?

OUR religious laws do not stipulate what a bride or groom must wear. However, interesting customs have developed over the years.

The Talmud often compares a bride and groom to a king and queen. In those times, the bride and groom were often seated on throne-like chairs, wearing crowns and wreaths as part of their regal costume.

Jews in each country have developed their own particular style of wedding dress. In some countries, the dress is very ornate. Jewish brides in Iraq, for example, wear silver bells and golden nose rings. In Arab countries, Jewish brides wear necklaces and headdresses of gold and silver.

The most common custom among Jews with an Eastern European tradition, as among the general American population, is for a bride to wear white, a symbol of purity. The bride wears a veil at the ceremony, reminiscent of the Biblical Rebeccah who covered her face when she first saw her future husband Isaac.

For the groom, the traditional custom is to wear a *kittel*, a simple white robe, over his wedding suit, which denotes purity, humility and festivity.

In selecting your own wedding attire, keep in mind that Judaism frowns upon needless extravagance. Modesty is very much in keeping with our tradition.

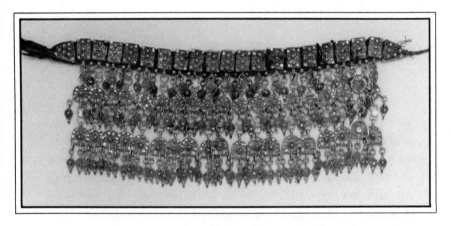

This Yemenite silver bridal necklace is composed of a row of rectangular plaques backed with fabric and hung with elaborate pendants.

"By this ring are you consecrated unto me."
WEDDING CEREMONY

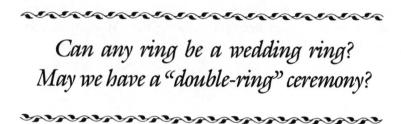

Can any ring be a wedding ring? May we have a "double-ring" ceremony?

THE giving and accepting of an item of value in the presence of witnesses is the most important part of the Jewish wedding ceremony. In earlier times, coins were used as the preferred object of exchange. Each country had its own custom as to how a bride was to accept the gift. For example, brides in Baghdad wore silk gloves to demonstrate that their acceptance of the coin was not to be construed as charity.

It has become almost universal Jewish practice, with the exception of only a few Oriental communities, to use a ring as the token of the marriage bond. Just as a ring has no beginning and no end, so too it is the wish of every bride and groom that their love be complete and unending.

Jewish law states that every ring must meet three standards:
- It must belong to the groom.
- It must be of solid metal, customarily gold.
- It cannot have gems or stones in it.

One ring, given by the groom to his bride, is required. However, double-ring ceremonies in which both bride and groom exchange rings, can usually take place in Reform and Conservative weddings. While the gift of coins or a ring was originally conceived as a token of acquisition, the double exchange of rings expresses, in a contemporary setting, a partnership, with a mutuality of respect and an equality of status.

Be sure to consult with your rabbi before purchasing your ring(s).

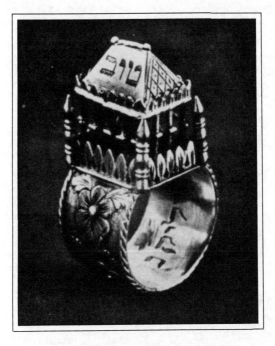

Elaborate gold marriage ring with miniature building at the top carrying the Hebrew inscription Mazal tov *(good luck).*

בס׳ מנא טבא ובמזלא מעליא

Elaborate ketubbot *were used in Italy beginning in the sixteenth century. They were often illuminated with compositions of fruits, flowers and birds.*
Illuminated Parchment Marriage Contract, Livorno, Italy 1748

> "Be thou my wife according to
> the law of Moses and Israel."
>
> KETUBAH

What is the ketubah?
If we have a ketubah, do we also need
a civil marriage license?

THE *ketubah* is a Jewish legal document. It confirms the religious bonds of your union. It does not take the place of a standard civil marriage license, which the rabbi will need in order to perform the ceremony.

The *ketubah,* in one form or another, has been used by Jews for more than two thousand years. The traditional *ketubah* is written in Aramaic, the language of the Jews exiled in Babylonia. The earliest formulation of the *ketubah* is found in the Talmud. It was written by Shimon ben Shetach, president of the ancient rabbinic court. Two thousand years later, we still use his words. The great innovation of the Jewish marriage document is its recognition that not only love, but also legal commitment is necessary in a Jewish marriage.

The husband's primary obligations are listed in the *ketubah.* He must cherish and honor his wife, provide for her support and sexual fulfillment. His financial obligations in case of divorce are also spelled out to insure the woman sufficient funds should the marriage be terminated.

·⟦ 25 ⟧·

Many new *ketubot* include two parallel declarations of commitment by both bride and groom.

The *ketubah* can be a beautiful work of art. Should you decide to join the growing number of couples who have a *ketubah* designed especially for them, be sure to commission an artist well in advance so that it will be ready in time for your wedding day. The artist must also confer with your rabbi as to the exact wording and variable spellings of Hebrew names and places that will appear in your *ketubah*.

Two witnesses are required for the signing of the *ketubah*. They sign the *ketubah* in Hebrew. Jewish law requires that legal witnesses be adult, religiously observant, and not related by blood or marriage to either the bride or groom or to each other. The officiating rabbi and cantor can serve as witnesses unless they are related to the bride or groom. Orthodox rabbis will allow only males to serve as witnesses. Reform and some Conservative rabbis will permit women to participate. Since your witnesses will be asked to sign their complete names in Hebrew, remind them to prepare for this requirement. To serve as a witness to a Jewish marriage is an honor and an important responsibility. Do choose your witnesses carefully.

"God creates new worlds constantly
by causing marriages to take place."

ZOHAR 1:89a

What is the ḥuppah, and what does it symbolize?

A ḤUPPAH is the wedding canopy under which the bride and groom stand during the marriage ceremony. (It is optional at Reform weddings.) The *ḥuppah* symbolizes the home that the bride and groom will create as husband and wife.

The wedding canopy has an interesting history. In Biblical times the meaning of the word *ḥuppah* was "room" or "covering." The Book of Joel states: "Let the bridegroom go forth from his chamber and the bride out of her pavilion (*ḥuppah*)."

During the rabbinic era, the *ḥuppah* referred to the bridal chamber erected by the groom's father and covered with purple cloth, a sign of royalty. Centuries later, when outdoor weddings became very popular, the *ḥuppah* took the form of a portable fabric canopy, rather than a fixed structure.

In ancient Israel, it was also customary to plant a tree on the occasion of the birth of a child. When the child married, the branches from that tree were used as poles and the leaves as decoration for the wedding canopy.

Among Sephardic Jews and some German Jews it is customary to drape a large prayer shawl, *tallit,* around the bride and groom.

Today, wedding canopies are available in many sizes, colors and styles. Some are made from fiber, others are floral. A *ḥuppah* can be as simple as a *tallit* held up by four poles, or quite elaborate. Be sure to inquire about the canopy which will be used at your wedding ceremony. If you want the *ḥuppah* decorated with flowers or greenery, inform your florist. Some synagogues and reception halls have several *ḥuppah* styles from which to choose. Like the other choices you will be making, your selection of a particular style of *ḥuppah* can reflect your own tastes.

*From the sixteenth century on, Jewish weddings were
often held outdoors. The couple in this engraving stand
under a* tallit *before the wall of the synagogue.*
NUPTIAL CEREMONY OF THE GERMAN JEWS
DuBosc after Bernard Picart

"Sing unto the Lord with the harp...
With trumpets and sound of cornet
make a joyful noise..."

PSALM 98:4-6

What kind of music shall we choose?

MUSIC, with its power to elicit strong expressions of joy and tender expressions of love, has always been an integral part of the Jewish wedding ceremony and celebration. Even in Biblical times, marriage processions were often accompanied by musicians. And later, in Talmudic times, some rabbis would lead the wedding guests in responsive singing.

In choosing the music for your wedding ceremony, you have an opportunity to fashion a unique and meaningful setting. There are many Jewish folk, liturgical and even modern melodies from which to choose. If you do not have the knowledge to make educated choices, be sure to consult with the cantor of your synagogue. The traditional American "Here Comes the Bride" is usually avoided, as it was composed by Wagner, a known anti-Semite. By selecting music which echoes our Jewish heritage, you can transform your ceremonial march down the aisle into a beautiful and moving experience.

The music at the party following the ceremony can range from the single voice of one acoustical or electronic instrument to the collective sound of a small band or a large orchestra. The size of the room and the number of guests are important factors to consider. Decide on the kind of mood you would like to create. If you plan a quiet, intimate party, where conversation among your guests is of primary concern, a single musician or a few strolling violinists might be your choice. If, on the other hand, you want an upbeat affair with dancing as the main focus, a band with a strong rhythm section might suit you better.

The inclusion of Israeli and traditional Jewish wedding dances always adds a large measure of *freilichkeit* (joyousness) to a wedding celebration. When you interview musicians, be sure to ask if this music is in their repertoire. If the director is not familiar with any particular selection you want played, you may provide a recording or sheet music a few weeks in advance.

"My soul takes pleasure in three things,
for they are beautiful to the Lord and to all men:
harmony among brothers, friendship among neighbors,
and a husband and wife suited to each other."

BEN SIRA 25:1

What are tenaim?

YEARS ago most Jewish marriages were arranged through a matchmaker, a *shadchan*. The practice dates back to Biblical times. In the Book of Genesis we read how Abraham's servant was sent on a mission to find an appropriate bride for Isaac. His search was successful, and Rebeccah, who stood out because of her extreme kindness, became Isaac's bride and Judaism's second matriarch.

In Talmudic times, as soon as a match was arranged, the parents of the bride and groom negotiated the terms of the dowry. These terms were set forth in a contract called *tenaim*, which means "stipulations." This contract was legally binding, and a fine or penalty was imposed if either party reneged on the arrangement. In European communities, the *tenaim* were often officially sealed by breaking a dinner plate, an act which corresponds to the breaking of the glass at the wedding ceremony. Eastern communities developed other traditions surrounding the *tenaim,* often including the exchange of gifts.

Today, although some still practice these customs, we are not required to set forth *tenaim*. And because arranged marriages are less common in our time, the ceremony has lost its popularity. It is interesting that some couples have reinterpreted the practice by formalizing a pre-nuptial contract relating to the couple's life together. It can include the desired number of children, finances, professional careers, the role of religion, and so forth.

It was customary for the bride and groom to exchange presents on the evening before their wedding. Prayer books with silver bindings were popular gifts. This German silver covered prayerbook dates from the mid-18th century.

"Praised be Thou, O Lord,
who bestows joy upon groom and bride."

SHEVA BRACHOT

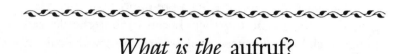

What is the aufruf?

THE *aufruf* ceremony is a unique occasion to honor the groom and his bride. The word *aufruf* is derived from the German, meaning "calling up." It refers to the "calling up" of the groom-to-be, and in liberal congregations the bride as well, to the Torah for an *aliyah*. The origin of the custom of *aufruf* is ascribed to King Solomon who, it is told, had his attendants perform kindnesses for a groom on the Sabbath preceding his wedding day.

Today, the *aufruf* gives public recognition to a forthcoming marriage. We take joy and pride in welcoming the newest Jewish family-to-be to the community.

The *aufruf* is usually scheduled on the Sabbath immediately prior to the wedding. If that Sabbath is inconvenient, the *aufruf* can take place on an earlier Sabbath or during a weekday service when the Torah is read (Monday, Thursday and Rosh Ḥodesh). The *aufruf* can be held in the synagogue of either the bride or the groom. If neither family is affiliated with a synagogue, arrangements can be made by contacting a local congregation.

When the groom is called up to the Torah for an *aliyah,* he recites the following blessing:

·⟦ 34 ⟧·

The person called to the Torah:

בָּרְכוּ אֶת יְיָ הַמְבֹרָךְ.

Barechu et adonai ham'vorach.

Congregation:

בָּרוּךְ יְיָ הַמְבֹרָךְ לְעוֹלָם וָעֶד.

Baruch adonai ham'vorach l'olam va-ed.

The person repeats the response and continues:

בָּרוּךְ אַתָּה, יְיָ אֱלֹהֵינוּ, מֶלֶךְ הָעוֹלָם, אֲשֶׁר בָּחַר
בָּנוּ מִכָּל הָעַמִּים, וְנָתַן לָנוּ אֶת תּוֹרָתוֹ. בָּרוּךְ אַתָּה,
יְיָ, נוֹתֵן הַתּוֹרָה.

*Baruch atah adonai elohenu melech ha-olam asher baḥar
banu mikol ha-amim, v'natan lahnu et torahto.
Baruch atah adonai, notayn ha-torah.*

When Torah portion is completed:

בָּרוּךְ אַתָּה, יְיָ אֱלֹהֵינוּ, מֶלֶךְ הָעוֹלָם, אֲשֶׁר נָתַן
לָנוּ תּוֹרַת אֱמֶת, וְחַיֵּי עוֹלָם נָטַע בְּתוֹכֵנוּ. בָּרוּךְ
אַתָּה, יְיָ, נוֹתֵן הַתּוֹרָה.

*Baruch atah adonai elohenu melech ha-olam asher
natan lanu torat emet v'chayeh olam netah b'tochaynu.
Baruch atah adonai notayn ha-Torah.*

In many Conservative and Reform congregations the bride
shares her groom's *aliyah* or receives one of her own.

It may also be customary to offer honors to the parents and
grandparents of the bride and groom.

The rabbi may recite a prayer on behalf of the couple:

"May He who blessed our fathers Abraham, Isaac and Jacob, bless _____ ,
and his bride _____ ,

who are soon to be joined in marriage. May they be privileged to fashion a Jewish home harboring love and harmony, peace and companionship. May they be blessed with children reared in health and well-being, devoted to Torah and to good deeds."

Some congregations, following an old custom, throw nuts, raisins and candies after the groom's *aliyah* or after the rabbi blesses the couple. These foods symbolize the wish for a sweet and fruitful, prosperous life. This is a lovely, fun-filled custom to follow. Be aware, however, that candies sweet to the taste-buds can be painful when thrown to other parts of the face. It is a good idea to choose very soft candies and to wrap them so they may be eaten even if they land on the floor first.

At the conclusion of the Sabbath services, it is customary for the family of the groom and bride to invite the congregation to a *kiddush,* Sabbath refreshments. In this way, the *mitzvah* of hospitality is fulfilled and everyone present may share in the celebration.

"Whatever way one desires to go, one is led."
MAKKOT 10b

What is a mikvah?

WITH all the many demands made on you during this hectic time, it is natural to become caught up in the details of preparation. It is all too easy to forget the spiritual aspect of the momentous occasion which awaits you.

One way in which this spiritual need can be fulfilled is for the bride-to-be to go to the *mikvah,* the ritual bath, on a night preceding the wedding. *Mikvah* is a Hebrew term meaning "gathering of water." It is applied to the public ritual bath that has for centuries been maintained by every Jewish community. The use of a *mikvah* is a requirement of traditional Jewish law for the purpose of purification and cleanliness of the body. A matron will be present to guide the bride-to-be through the brief ritual, and to assist her. As a rule, *mikvah* attendants encourage a prospective bride to call for an appointment. In some Orthodox communities it is also customary for the groom to visit the *mikvah* on the morning of the wedding or on the Friday afternoon preceeding it.

Booklets discussing this topic in greater detail are available at the *mikvah* or from your rabbi.

18th century engraving of the mikvah *in Amsterdam*

"May our supplications rise at nightfall,
our prayers approach Thy presence from the dawn,
and let our exultation come at dusk."

HIGH HOLIDAY MAḤZOR

Why do some brides and grooms fast on their wedding day?

SOME brides and grooms fast on their wedding day until they share a sip of wine under the *ḥuppah*. The traditional feeling is that for them, this day is a kind of *Yom Kippur,* a day of contemplation of the past and a looking forward to the future. It is the finale of one kind of life, and the prelude to another. Just as fasting on *Yom Kippur* is meant to cleanse the soul, so too, abstaining from food on one's wedding day symbolizes the beginning of a new life and the cleansing of all one's past misdeeds.

What happens before the wedding ceremony begins?

BEFORE the start of the formal wedding ceremony, the *ketubah* is signed. By the symbolic act of *kinyan,* the groom accepts a material object from the rabbi, usually a handkerchief, lifts it, and then returns it. In this way the groom demonstrates his willingness to fulfill his obligations as stipulated in the *ketubah.* The two witnesses then sign their names to the document.

There are variations in the customs related to the signing of the *ketubah.* Some Conservative and Reform rabbis have both bride and groom sign, each in the presence of the same two witnesses. In some Reform weddings, no provision is made for a *ketubah,* while in others a revised document is used.

Bedeken is the veiling ceremony. It is generally not a Reform custom. During the *bedeken,* the groom comes to officially "claim" his bride. The groom lowers the veil over his bride's face. According to one interpretation, this veiling ceremony developed to prevent a recurrence of what happened to Jacob in Biblical times. You will remember that Laban, Rachel's father, tricked the groom Jacob by substituting his older daughter, Leah, who wore an opaque veil. In order to avoid Jacob's dilemma, it has become customary for the groom to personally lower the veil over his bride's face. Others view the veiling of the bride as an act of modesty, as Rebeccah veiled herself when she first met Isaac, her betrothed.

After the bride is veiled, the groom or the bride's father recites the blessing given to Rebeccah by her mother and brother before she left to marry Isaac: "Our sister, be thou the mother of thousands, of ten thousands." This blessing is often followed by the Priestly Blessing: "May God bless you and keep you. May God shine His countenance upon you and be gracious unto you. May God turn His presence toward you and favor you with peace."

The wedding ceremony will begin in but a moment.

Through primarily a legal document stating the obligations of the groom to his bride, the ketubah *is often a work of art. This modern Reform interpretation uses Hebrew calligraphy and illumination.*

"Come now in peace, our bride whom we woo,
Come with rejoicing as gladsome guest
Crowning your people faithful and true..."
LECHAH DODI

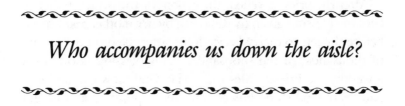

Who accompanies us down the aisle?

THE custom of escorting the bride and groom to the *ḥuppah* is an ancient one. An early Midrashic story attributes the practice to God, who was described as "bringing" Eve to Adam. Throughout Jewish history brides and grooms have been compared to kings and queens, who always appear with an entourage. The tradition of attendants continues to this day. It is a great joy for parents, grandparents, sisters, brothers and close friends to lead the bride and groom to their wedding canopy.

The order of the procession and the number of participants is not fixed by Jewish law. Some customs have continued over the years, and these may help serve as guides.

Since Judaism has always emphasized the important role of parents, it is most usual for bride and groom to be escorted by both their parents.

The role of the best man and maid or matron of honor has an early precedent. Legend has it that Michael and Gabriel, two angels, attended the wedding of Adam and Eve. They are considered the prototypical friends of the bride and groom.

The groom's friends might be in charge of the ring(s). The bride's friends may be asked to hold the *ketubah* and help lift the veil when the bride sips the wine. Grandparents and siblings may also join the processional. Older participants may be seated during the ceremony.

At the conclusion of the wedding ceremony, the bride and groom walk up the aisle together, followed, in reverse order, by those who participated in the processional.

Some couples hold a rehearsal a few days before the wedding. This is not at all necessary. If the attendants arrive before the other guests, a brief rehearsal can be held then. This should prove sufficient time to create a dignified wedding processional.

A JEWISH WEDDING
Oil on canvas by Mourycy Gottlieb (1856–1879)

What are the parts of the wedding ceremony, and what do they mean?

THE Jewish wedding ceremony began to take its present form in the 11th century. Prior to that time, marriage was accomplished in two separate rituals which took place approximately a year apart.

The first ritual was a betrothal ceremony known as *erusin*. It differed from the modern concept of engagement. A formal bill of divorce was required if *erusin* was broken. After the betrothal ceremony, the couple set their wedding date. The bride returned to her father's house for a period of about one year. This allowed the groom additional time to learn a trade so that he could be better prepared to provide financial support for his family.

The second ritual was known as *nisuin*. This was the name given to the formal wedding ceremony.

Over time, the *erusin* and *nisuin* ceremonies began to take place on the same day. The modern Jewish wedding ceremony still shows the seam where the two rituals were joined; the presence of two cups of wine, or in some cases one cup filled twice, is a reminder of the time when two separate occasions were celebrated.

In some European communities it was customary for the bride, as she arrived at the *huppah,* to circle the groom seven times (an alternative custom was three times). The exact origin of this custom is unclear. Some believe that its purpose was to ward off evil spirits. Others saw the number seven as symbolic of perfection, since the world was created in seven days. Today the circling of the groom is an optional ritual rarely seen in Conservative and Reform ceremonies.

Most rabbis begin the formal wedding ceremony by welcoming the bride and groom and the assembled guests. This is followed by a prayer for God's blessing:

בָּרוּךְ הַבָּא בְּשֵׁם יְיָ.

May you who are here be blessed in the name of the Lord.

Huppah *stone, the special stone on which the glass-breaking of the wedding takes place.* Huppah *stones were put in the north wall of synagogues. The one above is from the German synagogue at Altenkundstadt.*

Wine is always associated with Jewish celebrations. In Orthodox and Conservative wedding ceremonies it is customary to use two cups of wine. Reform ceremonies will often have a single cup of wine. The cups are placed on a small table under the *huppah*. The *erusin* are celebrated with two blessings:

בָּרוּךְ אַתָּה, יְיָ אֱלֹהֵינוּ, מֶלֶךְ הָעוֹלָם,
בּוֹרֵא פְּרִי הַגָּפֶן.

Praised be Thou, O Lord our God, King of the universe, who createst the fruit of the vine.

This is followed by another blessing thanking God for making the couple holy by sanctifying marriage:

בָּרוּךְ אַתָּה, יְיָ אֱלֹהֵינוּ, מֶלֶךְ הָעוֹלָם, אֲשֶׁר
קִדְּשָׁנוּ בְּמִצְוֹתָיו וְצִוָּנוּ עַל הָעֲרָיוֹת, וְאָסַר לָנוּ אֶת
הָאֲרוּסוֹת, וְהִתִּיר לָנוּ אֶת הַנְּשׂוּאוֹת לָנוּ עַל יְדֵי
חֻפָּה וְקִדּוּשִׁין. בָּרוּךְ אַתָּה, יְיָ, מְקַדֵּשׁ עַמּוֹ יִשְׂרָאֵל
עַל יְדֵי חֻפָּה וְקִדּוּשִׁין.

Praised be Thou O Lord, who hallowest Thy people Israel with the *huppah* and the rites of matrimony.

The bride and groom now drink from the first cup of wine. The groom then places the ring on his bride's right index finger. There are several explanations for the selection of this particular finger. Some ascribe a direct lifeline from this finger to the heart. Others explain that this is the finger which points to heaven, the source of all. Still others more practically assert that this finger is not generally accustomed to receiving a ring, and so its placement is not likely to be unintentional. Following the ceremony, the ring may be moved to the more usual "ring finger." Some rabbis have the ring placed on the finger where it will be normally worn.

As the groom places the ring on his bride's finger, he recites the traditional words of consecration:

הֲרֵי אַתְּ מְקֻדֶּשֶׁת לִי בְּטַבַּעַת זוֹ כְּדַת מֹשֶׁה וְיִשְׂרָאֵל.

Haray aht m'kudeshet li b'taba'at zoh k'dat moshe v'yisrael.

By this ring you are consecrated to me as my wife in accordance with the Law of Moses and the people Israel.

In a double ring ceremony, the bride then gives her groom a ring and might recite:

הֲרֵי אַתָּה מְקֻדָּשׁ לִי בְּטַבַּעַת זוֹ כְּדַת מֹשֶׁה וְיִשְׂרָאֵל.

Haray ahtah m'kudash li b'taba'at zoh
k'dat moshe v'yisrael.

By this ring you are consecrated to me as my husband in accordance with the Law of Moses and the people of Israel.

or

אֲנִי לְדוֹדִי וְדוֹדִי לִי

Ahni l'dodi v'dodi li.

I am my beloved's and my beloved is mine.

Some couples add a favorite poem or a personal statement during the exchange of rings. You might discuss this possibility with your rabbi.

The ring ceremony completes the first part of the wedding ceremony.

There are no formal vows in the Jewish wedding liturgy. However, some rabbis do include vows immediately following the exchange of rings:

Do you, ————————————————— ,

take —————————————————————

to be your husband/bride, promising to protect and cherish him/her, whether in good fortune or in adversity, and to seek together a life hallowed by the faith of Israel?

Some Conservative and Reform rabbis may permit the recitation of your own written vows during this part of the ceremony.

The rabbi now reads either all or a portion of the *ketubah*. It is then given to the groom, who gives it to his bride. The bride, who will have permanent possession of the document, may give it to her parents or to an attendant for temporary safekeeping.

German silver Double Marriage Cup, late 19th century.
Wedding cups were often commissioned for
use during the wedding ceremony.

After the *ketubah* reading, some rabbis make a personal statement to the bride and groom. Others may deliver a brief message about marriage in general. You may wish to discuss the content of this presentation with your rabbi, perhaps sharing personal anecdotes or other information that might be included.

The recitation of the Seven Blessings of Marriage (*Sheva Brachot*) follows. The blessings are usually recited by the rabbi or cantor. Sometimes close friends or relatives of the bride and groom are invited to recite the blessings. Each blessing can be followed by a personal wish for the bride and groom.

בָּרוּךְ אַתָּה, יְיָ אֱלֹהֵינוּ, מֶלֶךְ הָעוֹלָם, בּוֹרֵא פְּרִי הַגָּפֶן.

בָּרוּךְ אַתָּה, יְיָ אֱלֹהֵינוּ, מֶלֶךְ הָעוֹלָם, שֶׁהַכֹּל בָּרָא לִכְבוֹדוֹ.

בָּרוּךְ אַתָּה, יְיָ אֱלֹהֵינוּ, מֶלֶךְ הָעוֹלָם, יוֹצֵר הָאָדָם.

בָּרוּךְ אַתָּה, יְיָ אֱלֹהֵינוּ, מֶלֶךְ הָעוֹלָם, אֲשֶׁר יָצַר אֶת הָאָדָם בְּצַלְמוֹ, בְּצֶלֶם דְּמוּת תַּבְנִיתוֹ, וְהִתְקִין לוֹ מִמֶּנּוּ בִּנְיַן עֲדֵי עַד. בָּרוּךְ אַתָּה, יְיָ, יוֹצֵר הָאָדָם.

שׂוֹשׂ תָּשִׂישׂ וְתָגֵל הָעֲקָרָה, בְּקִבּוּץ בָּנֶיהָ לְתוֹכָהּ בְּשִׂמְחָה. בָּרוּךְ אַתָּה, יְיָ, מְשַׂמֵּחַ צִיּוֹן בְּבָנֶיהָ.

שַׂמֵּחַ תְּשַׂמַּח רֵעִים הָאֲהוּבִים, כְּשַׂמֵּחֲךָ יְצִירְךָ בְּגַן עֵדֶן מִקֶּדֶם. בָּרוּךְ אַתָּה יְיָ, מְשַׂמֵּחַ חָתָן וְכַלָּה.

בָּרוּךְ אַתָּה, יְיָ אֱלֹהֵינוּ, מֶלֶךְ הָעוֹלָם, אֲשֶׁר בָּרָא שָׂשׂוֹן וְשִׂמְחָה, חָתָן וְכַלָּה, גִּילָה רִנָּה דִּיצָה וְחֶדְוָה, אַהֲבָה וְאַחֲוָה וְשָׁלוֹם וְרֵעוּת, מְהֵרָה יְיָ אֱלֹהֵינוּ

יִשָּׁמַע בְּעָרֵי יְהוּדָה וּבְחוּצוֹת יְרוּשָׁלַיִם קוֹל שָׂשׂוֹן,
וְקוֹל שִׂמְחָה, קוֹל חָתָן וְקוֹל כַּלָּה, קוֹל מִצְהֲלוֹת
חֲתָנִים מֵחֻפָּתָם, וּנְעָרִים מִמִּשְׁתֵּה נְגִינָתָם. בָּרוּךְ
אַתָּה יְיָ, מְשַׂמֵּחַ חָתָן עִם הַכַּלָּה.

Praised be Thou, O Lord our God, King of the universe, who createst the fruit of the vine.

Praised be Thou, O Lord our God, King of the universe, who hast created all things for Thy glory.

Praised be Thou, O Lord our God, King of the universe, Creator of man.

Praised be Thou, O Lord our God, King of the universe, who hast fashioned man in Thine own image, after Thine own likeness, and hast established through him an enduring edifice of life. Praised be Thou, O Lord, Creator of man.

May Zion, who has been made barren of her children, soon rejoice as her children return joyfully unto her. Praised be Thou, O Lord, who causest Zion to rejoice at the return of her children.

Bestow abundant joy to the beloved companions as Thou didst bestow joy upon the first man and wife in the Garden of Eden. Praised be Thou, O Lord, who bestowest joy upon groom and bride.

Praised be Thou, O Lord our God, King of the universe, who hast created joy and gladness, a groom and his bride, mirth and exultation, dancing and jubilation, love and harmony, peace and companionship. O Lord our God, may there soon be heard again in the cities of Judah and in the streets of Jerusalem, glad and joyous voices, the voices of groom and bride, the jubilant voices of those joined in marriage under the *ḥupah,* the voices of young people feasting and singing. Praised be Thou, O Lord, who causest the groom to rejoice with his bride.

The bride and groom now drink from the second cup of wine.

Some rabbis end the wedding ceremony with the official pronouncement: "By the power vested in me . . . you are now husband and wife."

Others bless the bride and groom with the threefold priestly benediction:

יְבָרֶכְךָ יְיָ וְיִשְׁמְרֶךָ.

יָאֵר יְיָ פָּנָיו אֵלֶיךָ וִיחֻנֶּךָּ.

יִשָּׂא יְיָ פָּנָיו אֵלֶיךָ וְיָשֵׂם לְךָ שָׁלוֹם.

May the Lord bless you and keep you.
May the Lord show you favor and be gracious unto you.
May the Lord show you kindness and give you peace.

At this point, the groom smashes a wrapped glass with his foot. This ancient custom has been given a variety of interpretations. One, dating back to Talmudic times, speaks of Rabbi Mar de-Rabina who felt that his disciples had become too frivolous at the wedding of his son. He grabbed a costly glass and threw it to the ground. This had a sobering effect on the guests. His message was that where there is celebration, there should also be awe and trembling. A related interpretation sees the breaking of the glass as a reminder of the destruction of the Temple in Jerusalem.

This somber reflection lasts for just an instant. Shouts of *mazal tov* greet the sound of shattered glass. Music and spontaneous hand clapping greet the newly married couple as they leave the *ḥuppah*.

Following the recessional, the bride and groom spend a few moments alone. This is called *yiḥud* and began in ancient times when the groom brought his bride to his tent to consummate the marriage. It is customary for the bride and groom to break their fast during *yiḥud,* sharing their first food as husband and wife.

After your wedding ceremony, do share a few moments alone together before returning to greet your guests. These precious minutes can be memorable and lasting. The *yiḥud* experience will give you a peaceful time for shared reflection. The bride's room or the rabbi's study will be made available to you.

The *nisuin* are now complete.

"Go eat your bread with gladness and
drink your wine with a joyous heart."
ECCLESIASTES 9:7

Are there religious observances related to the wedding reception?

THE reception following the wedding ceremony is truly a *simḥa,* an occasion of great joy. The celebration is so important in Jewish tradition that the Talmud tells us even the study of Torah must be interrupted to bring joy and honor to newlyweds.

At the wedding feast, singing, dancing and merrymaking are the rule. The bride and groom are often lifted on chairs and carried around the room. It is a religious commandment, a *mitzvah,* to rejoice with the bride and groom.

The wedding reception is traditionally ended with the recitation of the Grace after Meals, *Birkat Hamazon.* In the special Grace for weddings, the seven blessings recited under the *ḥupah* are recited once again. Friends of the bride and groom can be honored with the recitation of selected blessings. Two cups of wine are then poured together into a third cup. The bride and groom both drink from this cup in symbolic acceptance of the joining of the streams of their lives.

It is nice to remember the less fortunate at times of celebration. You might arrange to share your flowers with hospital patients and left over foods with the needy in your community.

"By wisdom is a house built, and
by understanding it is established."
PROVERBS 24:3

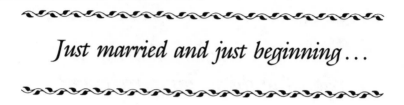

Just married and just beginning...

IN days gone by, brides and
grooms spent the first week of married life surrounded by
friends and relatives who fed and entertained them. This custom probably originated with the Biblical seven-day banquet
prepared by Laban for Jacob and Leah. Although more traditional couples still observe this custom, the honeymoon trip
usually displaces it.

Since Biblical times, the special status of a bride and groom
lasted for one complete year. The Book of Deuteronomy in-
forms us: "When a man takes a wife, he shall be deferred from
military duty . . . He shall be free for his house one year and
shall cheer his wife whom he has taken" (24:5). The first year of
every marriage presents a host of decisions and adjustments,
bringing with them tension and stress. Judaism's advice to
newlyweds is clearly to stay at home and learn to live with one
another.

When you marry you become the newest Jewish family in
your community. Jewish history begins with the family. Many
stories in the Bible deal with family histories. There are
the examples of the filial obedience of Isaac, the love of Jacob
for Rachel, the bond of friendship between Ruth and her
mother-in-law Naomi. These, and many others, give testi-

mony to family affection and the unique quality of Jewish family life.

Traditionally, an important goal of every Jewish family is to create an atmosphere of peace, *shalom bayit*. A Jewish home nurtures and promotes togetherness, cooperation and respect.

As a Jewish family, you can enrich your life with the symbolic objects and ritual acts of Judaism. Together you can celebrate the holy days of the Jewish year as well as the personal life cycle events of your family. May you have a lifetime together filled with joyous celebration!

Haggadah—15th century Spain
Matzah Plate and Elijah Cup—19th century Poland

A BEGINNING GUIDE TO HOME OBSERVANCE

JUDAISM is primarily a home-focused way of life. Each holiday, with its home symbols, rituals, foods, music and tales can bring delight to your family and, in turn, beauty and joy to living as a Jew.

The Jewish home is referred to as a *mikdash me'at,* a miniature sanctuary. A sanctuary or shelter is marked by tranquility and holiness. The kind of sanctuary you will build together depends on the choices you will make.

On the following pages you will find some of our most basic home rituals. They will help start you on your way.

When you recite the blessings, try to follow the precise Hebrew form as it has been handed down for generations. If you cannot read the Hebrew, you can use the transliteration provided underneath each Hebrew text. You will soon find comfort in repeating the same structures again and again, Shabbat after Shabbat, holiday after holiday, year after year. They can help you bring into your home the values and customs which have helped the Jewish family and the Jewish people to endure.

"Inscribe them on the doorposts
of your house, and on your gates."

DEUTERONOMY 6:9

Affixing the Mezuzah

Jewish homes are dedicated by affixing a mezuzah to the doorposts of the house. The mezuzah consists of a container made of wood, metal, stone, or ceramic containing a parchment scroll. Two passages from the Torah are lettered on the front of the scroll (Deuteronomy 6:4-9 and 11:13-21). The word *Shaddai* (Almighty) is lettered on the back. Usually this word can be seen through a hole in the container. Otherwise, the container often has the word or the Hebrew letter *shin* displayed on its front.

The mezuzah is affixed on the right-hand side as one enters. It is attached within the upper third of the doorpost. It is fastened diagonally, the top slanted toward the house. Before affixing the mezuzah say this blessing:

בָּרוּךְ אַתָּה, יְיָ אֱלֹהֵינוּ, מֶלֶךְ הָעוֹלָם, אֲשֶׁר קִדְּשָׁנוּ בְּמִצְוֹתָיו וְצִוָּנוּ לִקְבֹּעַ מְזוּזָה.

Baruch atah adonai elohenu melech ha-olam asher kidshanu b'mitzvotav v'tzivanu likboah mezuzah.

Blessed are You, Lord our God, Ruler of the universe,
who has made us holy by giving us His commandments,
and has commanded us to affix the mezuzah.

"Come let us welcome the Sabbath.
May its radiance illumine our hearts
as we kindle these tapers."
THE UNION PRAYER BOOK

Lighting the Shabbat Candles

Sabbath candles may be lit, at the earliest, 1 1/4 hours before sunset, but the usual time is up to 18 minutes before sunset.

Light the candles.

Move your hands around the flames several times and bring them toward your face. This gesture symbolically welcomes the Sabbath into your home.

Place your hands over your eyes, so that you will not see the Sabbath lights until you have recited the blessing.

בָּרוּךְ אַתָּה, יְיָ אֱלֹהֵינוּ, מֶלֶךְ הָעוֹלָם, אֲשֶׁר
קִדְּשָׁנוּ בְּמִצְוֹתָיו וְצִוָּנוּ לְהַדְלִיק נֵר שֶׁל שַׁבָּת.

*Baruch atah adonai elohenu melech ha-olam asher kidshanu
b'mitzvotav v'tzivanu l'hadlik ner shel shabbat.*

Blessed are You, Lord our God, Ruler of the universe,
who has made us holy by giving us His commandments,
and has commanded us to kindle the Sabbath lights.

> "In love and favor thou has given us
> the holy Sabbath as a heritage,
> a reminder of Thy work of creation,
> first of our sacred days."

SABBATH KIDDUSH

Kiddush
(Blessing over Wine)

Hold the wine cup in your right hand as you recite the blessings:

בָּרוּךְ אַתָּה, יְיָ אֱלֹהֵינוּ, מֶלֶךְ הָעוֹלָם, בּוֹרֵא פְּרִי הַגָּפֶן.

Baruch atah adonai elohenu melech ha-olam
boray p'ri ha-gafen.

Blessed are You, Lord our God, Ruler of the universe,
who creates the fruit of the vine.

בָּרוּךְ אַתָּה, יְיָ אֱלֹהֵינוּ, מֶלֶךְ הָעוֹלָם, אֲשֶׁר קִדְּשָׁנוּ בְּמִצְוֹתָיו וְרָצָה בָנוּ וְשַׁבַּת קָדְשׁוֹ בְּאַהֲבָה וּבְרָצוֹן הִנְחִילָנוּ, זִכָּרוֹן לְמַעֲשֵׂה בְרֵאשִׁית. כִּי הוּא יוֹם תְּחִלָּה לְמִקְרָאֵי קֹדֶשׁ, זֵכֶר לִיצִיאַת מִצְרָיִם. כִּי־בָנוּ בָחַרְתָּ וְאוֹתָנוּ קִדַּשְׁתָּ מִכָּל־הָעַמִּים, וְשַׁבַּת קָדְשְׁךָ בְּאַהֲבָה וּבְרָצוֹן הִנְחַלְתָּנוּ.

Blessed are You, Lord our God, Ruler of the universe. You have made us holy by giving us Your commandments and have shown us Your favor. With love You have given us Your holy Sabbath which recalls the work of Creation. This day is the first of the holy festivals recalling our going forth from Egypt. You have chosen us from all peoples, and You have shown us Your loving favor by giving us Your holy Sabbath.

בָּרוּךְ אַתָּה, יְיָ, מְקַדֵּשׁ הַשַׁבָּת.

Baruch atah adonai m'kadesh ha-shabbat.

Blessed are You, who makes the Sabbath holy.

Ha-Motzi
(Blessing over Bread)

בָּרוּךְ אַתָּה, יְיָ אֱלֹהֵינוּ, מֶלֶךְ הָעוֹלָם, הַמּוֹצִיא לֶחֶם מִן הָאָרֶץ.

*Baruch atah adonai elohenu melech ha-olam
ha-motzi leḥem min ha-aretz.*

Blessed are You, Lord our God, Ruler of the universe,
who brings forth bread from the earth.

"Yours the message cheering that the time is nearing
which will see all men free, tyrants disappearing."
ROCK OF AGES (HANUKKAH HYMN)

Lighting the Ḥanukkah Candles

As you face the Ḥanukkah Menorah, place the first candle
on your right. Subsequent candles are added to the left.
Light the shamash, take it in your hand and say:

בָּרוּךְ אַתָּה, יְיָ אֱלֹהֵינוּ, מֶלֶךְ הָעוֹלָם, אֲשֶׁר
קִדְּשָׁנוּ בְּמִצְוֹתָיו וְצִוָּנוּ לְהַדְלִיק נֵר שֶׁל חֲנֻכָּה.

Baruch atah adonai elohenu melech ha-olam asher kidshanu
b'mitzvotav v'tzivanu l'hadlik ner shel ḥanukkah.

Blessed are You, Lord our God, Ruler of the universe,
who has made us holy with His commandments
and has commanded us to kindle the Ḥanukkah lights.

בָּרוּךְ אַתָּה, יְיָ אֱלֹהֵינוּ, מֶלֶךְ הָעוֹלָם, שֶׁעָשָׂה
נִסִּים לַאֲבוֹתֵינוּ בַּיָּמִים הָהֵם בַּזְּמַן הַזֶּה.

Baruch atah adonai elohenu melech ha-olam she'asah
nisim la-avotaynu ba-yamim ha-hem bazman ha-zeh.

Blessed are You, Lord our God, Ruler of the universe,
who performed miracles for our ancestors
in long-ago days, at this season.

On the first night of Hanukkah, Sheheheyanu is also said:

בָּרוּךְ אַתָּה, יְיָ אֱלֹהֵינוּ, מֶלֶךְ הָעוֹלָם, שֶׁהֶחֱיָנוּ
וְקִיְמָנוּ וְהִגִיעָנוּ לַזְּמַן הַזֶּה.

*Baruch atah adonai elohenu melech ha-olam sheheheyanu
v'kiye-manu v'hi-gi-anu lazman ha-zeh.*

Blessed are You, Lord our God, Ruler of the Universe,
who has kept us alive and strong and
brought us to this season.

Light the candles. The new candle is always kindled first.

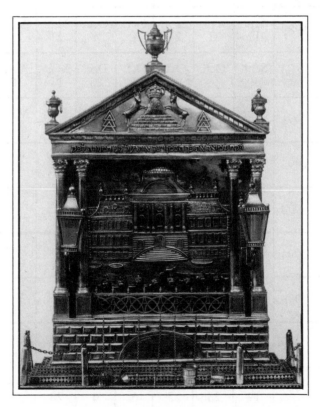

Hanukkah Lamp—Germany, 1814

SECULAR DATES OF JEWISH HOLIDAYS

DATES	Rosh Hashanah	Yom Kippur	Sukkot	Simhat Torah	Hanukkah	Purim	Passover	Shavuot
1988–1989	Sept. 12	Sept. 21	Sept. 26	Oct. 4	Dec. 4	Mar. 21	Apr. 20	June 9
1989–1990	Sept. 30	Oct. 9	Oct. 15	Oct. 22	Dec. 23	Mar. 11	Apr. 10	May 30
1990–1991	Sept. 20	Sept. 29	Oct. 4	Oct. 12	Dec. 12	Feb. 28	Mar. 30	May 19
1991–1992	Sept. 9	Sept. 18	Sept. 23	Oct. 1	Dec. 2	Mar. 19	Apr. 18	June 7
1992–1993	Sept. 28	Oct. 7	Oct. 12	Oct. 20	Dec. 20	Mar. 7	Apr. 6	May 26
1993–1994	Sept. 16	Sept. 25	Sept. 30	Oct. 8	Dec. 9	Feb. 25	Mar. 27	May 16
1994–1995	Sept. 6	Sept. 15	Sept. 20	Sept. 28	Nov. 28	Mar. 16	Apr. 15	June 4
1995–1996	Sept. 25	Oct. 4	Oct. 9	Oct. 17	Dec. 18	Mar. 5	Apr. 4	May 24
1996–1997	Sept. 14	Sept. 23	Sept. 28	Oct. 6	Dec. 6	Mar. 23	Apr. 22	June 11